DIY Crafts

2nd Edition

The 100 Most Popular Crafts & Projects That Make Your Life Easier, Keep You Entertained, And Help with Cleaning & Organizing!

by Kitty Moore

Copyright © 2017 By Kitty Moore
All rights reserved. No part of this book may be reproduced in any form without permission in writing from the author. No part of this publication may be reproduced or transmitted in any form or by any means, mechanic, electronic, photocopying, recording, by any storage or retrieval system, or transmitted by email without the permission in writing from the author and publisher.
For information regarding permissions write to author at kitty@artscraftsandmore.com.
Reviewers may quote brief passages in review.

Please note that credit for the images used in this book go to the respective owners. You can view this at: ArtsCraftsAndMore.com/image-list

Kitty Moore
ArtsCraftsAndMore.com

Table of Contents

Introduction — 7
1. Make Your Own Candles — 8
2. Pressed Flower Embellishments — 10
3. Make a Stunning Striped Cushion — 11
4. Easy French Knitting — 13
5. Re-Use Your Old Cookie Tins — 15
6. Mini Flower Pot Embellishments — 17
7. Trendy Key Holder — 18
8. Photo Blocks — 19
9. Fun Pillowcases — 20
10. Hot Pad with A Difference — 22
11. Coasters with A More Rustic Feel — 23
12. Make Plain Glassware Special — 24
13. Make Your Own Joy — 25
14. Pompom Mania — 26
15. Decorative Appliqué — 27
16. Stencil Crazy — 28
17. Coiled Bowls with A Difference — 29
18. Scrappy Spice — 30
19. Lovely Translucent Kite — 31
20. Pretty Easy Bracelet — 33
21. Scrubbies For Your Bath — 34
22. Family Memory Box — 35
23. Dried Flower Cards with A Difference — 36
24. Made in Minutes Flower Bouquet — 37

25. Upcycled Bottles _____ 38
26. Happy Cards _____ 39
27. A New Way to Decorate Clay Pots _____ 40
28. Memorable Gift Wrap _____ 41
29. Educational Butterfly Craft _____ 42
30. DIY Coloring Book _____ 44
31. Upcycled Egg Boxes _____ 45
32. Home Grown Crystals _____ 46
33. I Love a Ladybug Card _____ 47
34. Flowers Using Leftover Yarn _____ 48
35. Fun Fridge Cups _____ 49
36. Make Your Own Pump for Water Balloon Fights _____ 50
37. All Stitched Up _____ 51
38. Make Your Own Journal _____ 52
39. DIY Puff Paint _____ 53
40. Sunny Sun Macaroni Card _____ 55
41. Paper Tissue Flowers _____ 56
42. 4th of July Craft _____ 57
43. Make Yarn Fireworks for The 4th of July _____ 58
44. Little Family of Chickens _____ 59
45. Xmas Card Holder _____ 60
46. Plastic Fantasy Spoons _____ 61
47. Customized Cork Trivets _____ 62
48. Make Your Own Apple Embellishments _____ 63
49. Holiday Gift Toppers _____ 64
50. Personalized Wrapping Paper _____ 65
51. Make Your Own Dish Cloth _____ 66

52. *Easy Firework Craft* _____ *67*
53. *Waterfall for Your Pond* _____ *68*
54. *Sharpie Mug Craft* _____ *69*
55. *Upcycled Vases* _____ *70*
56. *A "Breath of Fresh Air" Wreath* _____ *71*
57. *Decorated Birdhouse* _____ *72*
58. *Gloved Doll* _____ *73*
59. *Winter Wonderland Bow* _____ *75*
60. *Festive Table Runner* _____ *76*
61. *Good Old-Fashioned Rock Candy* _____ *77*
62. *Retro Gift Labels* _____ *78*
63. *Planter Using an Old Tire* _____ *79*
64. *Update an Old Vase or Glass* _____ *80*
65. *Ombre Vase* _____ *81*
66. *Pretty Wooden Spoons* _____ *82*
67. *Fun Paper Project* _____ *83*
68. *Paper Bowl with A Difference* _____ *84*
69. *Natural Looking Bottles* _____ *85*
70. *Cute as A Button Magnets* _____ *86*
71. *Custom Paper Bouquet* _____ *87*
72. *Update Old Sunglasses* _____ *88*
73. *Easy Canvas Wall Art* _____ *89*
74. *Crayon Art with a Difference* _____ *90*
75. *Fun Noses for Dress Up* _____ *91*
76. *Retro Pinwheels* _____ *92*
77. *Keep Your Coffee Warm* _____ *93*
78. *Easy Origami Craft* _____ *94*

79. Make Your Own Jewelry Bead Cap _____ 95
80. Rainbow Tissue Flowers _____ 96
81. Festive Fall Napkin Ring _____ 97
82. Decorative Gift Envelope _____ 98
83. Durable Duct Tape Wallet _____ 99
84. 15-Minute Gift Bag _____ 100
85. Ombre Planter _____ 101
86. Easy Easter Floral Bouquet _____ 102
87. Gift Envelope for Gift Vouchers _____ 103
88. A Pretty Patterned Marquee Sign _____ 104
89. I Love You Bookmarks _____ 105
90. Quick Striped Canvas _____ 106
91. Updated Stone-Finished Pot _____ 107
92. Pretty Fairy Lights _____ 108
93. Brighten Your Potted Plants _____ 109
94. Cupcake Liner Flowers _____ 110
95. Beautiful Personalized Tags _____ 111
96. Swirl Embellishments _____ 112
97. Quick Stamps for Personal Projects _____ 113
98. Oak Tree Crafts _____ 114
99. Chicken Pix for Younger Kids _____ 115
100. Ribbon Embellishments _____ 116
Final Words _____ 117
Disclaimer _____ 118

Introduction

There is no need to sit on the couch all day watching TV just because you are bored. Get busy crafting! You will have great fun, and you can create a few pretty and useful items for your home or to use as gifts.

In this book, I have compiled my favorite crafts with all the instructions to ensure that they come out perfectly every time. Choose one or two that you like, or simply work your way through the whole book. There is definitely something for everyone in this compilation.

Well then, let's get started!

1. Make Your Own Candles

Materials

- A candle wick (at least 2 inches longer than the height of your candle)
- A mold (any container that can hold the wax will work)
- Wax (use candle wax or gather up bits of old candles or crayons)
- Double boiler (optional)
- A skewer

Directions

1. To start off, get the wick ready. Tie one end of the wick to the middle of the skewer. Now, melt the wax. This is best done in a double boiler over medium heat, but it can also be done in the microwave. If using the double boiler, stir the wax continuously until melted. If using the microwave, place on high for 30 seconds at a time, stirring after each session until melted completely.

2. Dip the free end of the wick into the wax, and quickly transfer to your container. Secure to the center of the bottom of the container while wax is still warm. (If necessary, use the skewer to help you position it properly).

3. Now you want to position the wick. Get two containers that are as long as your wick is now and set them on either side of the container you are using as a mold. Balance the skewer on these containers. What you want is to get the wick to stand as straight as possible.

4. Transfer the melted wax to your container, pouring it slowly so it doesn't splash out, and let it set. Depending on the thickness of your candle, this will take between 24-48 hours. Once the wax is set, cut the wick. Leave about ½ an inch protruding from the top of the candle. Then remove the candle from the mold.

2. Pressed Flower Embellishments

Materials

- Flowers from your garden (they should be in good shape and shouldn't be too fleshy- daisies are great for this)
- Four sheets of plain, white paper
- Three heavy books

Directions

1. Open up one of the books and lay down two of the sheets of paper on one side. Set out the flowers. Make sure they do not overlap. Put the other two pieces of paper over this. Your flowers will now be sandwiched between the four sheets of paper.

2. Close the book and then place the other books on top of it. Place the books where they will be undisturbed for at least a week. Check them after a week. If they are completely dry, they are ready for use.

3. Make a Stunning Striped Cushion

Materials

- A square of foam or a cushion pad
- ½ a yard of fabric that is at least 54 inches wide
- A coordinating sewing thread
- A sewing machine (you can also do this by hand, but it will take a lot longer)
- A rotary cutter and cutting mat or dressmaker's scissors
- Steel pins or gem clips to hold the fabric in place while you are sewing it

Directions

1. Cut out one square of fabric measuring 18.5" x 18.5". This will be the front piece. You will have two back pieces (so that there is a slit in the cushion) and they will take the shape of rectangles, each being 18.5" x 12.5".

2. Press under the first 1/8", along both of the long edges of your rectangle. Then press under a further inch of fabric. You need to fold it so that the wrong sides of the fabric face one another. Repeat with the other rectangle.

3. Lay the front piece down, with the right side facing up. Lay the first of the rectangles, right side facing down, over it

matching the 18.5" side with the edges of the square. Pin into place, allowing for a seam allowance of 1/8". Lay the second rectangle, right side facing down, in the same manner, matching the edges of the square. There should be an overlap in the middle. This will be so that you can remove the cushion inside. Press the seams open to set them, and turn the cover out so that the right side is showing. Press again if necessary.

4. Easy French Knitting

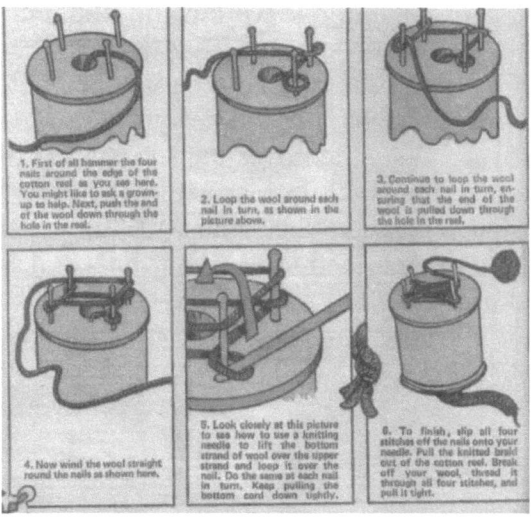

Materials

- A loom or doll made for French knitting
- Yarn in your choice of colors
- Crochet hook

Directions

1. Feed your yarn through the hole in the middle of the loom or doll. Wind your yarn around each of the pegs at the top. When viewed from the top, the yarn should form the shape of a U in relation to the peg next to it. Keep the yarn reasonably taut to maintain the tension, but keep in mind that you will have to pull this yarn over the hook, and this will be harder if it is too taut. Your working yarn should be on the outside of the peg. Wrap a second row of stitches.

2. Using a crochet hook, lift each of the first row of stitches up over the second row and off the peg. Wrap your next row of stitches, going in the same direction as before. Lift the next

group of stitches over again. Continue in this manner. The "knitting" will come out through the hole in the center at the bottom. Carry on until the work is the length that you desire.

3. Cast off by lifting the stitch on the first peg onto your crochet hook. Now carefully lift the second peg onto the hook as well. Lift the first stitch over the second and off the hook so there is just one stitch in place. Lift the yarn from the third peg on and repeat. Do the same with the fourth peg until all the yarn is off the loom/doll. Cut your yarn, leaving a short tail, and draw this tail through the stitch on the hook so that there are no more stitches on the hook. Draw tight to close the knot.

5. Re-Use Your Old Cookie Tins

Materials

- 3 different sized cookie tins
- Spray paint in the color of your choice (optional)
- Strong glue that will work on metal and wood
- Two lengths of dowelling rod (one about double the height of your biggest tin, the second about double the height of your second-biggest tin- they should be thick dowelling rods)

Directions

1. If you like the patterns on the cookie tins, leave them as they are and spray paint or varnish the dowelling rods. If you would rather paint the outside of the tins, do so now and set aside to dry. Starting with the biggest tin, find the center point inside the tin and glue your longest dowelling rod to this point. Leave to dry.

2. Take up the second-biggest tin and find the center point on both the inside and outside bottom of the tin. Glue the end of the first dowelling rod to the outside center of this tin and leave to dry. Glue your second dowelling rod to the center point at the inside of this tin and leave to dry.

3. Now, find the center point on the outside bottom of the smallest tin. Glue the second dowelling rod into place and set aside to dry. Add any embellishments that you like.

6. Mini Flower Pot Embellishments

Materials

- Polymer clay in the color of your choice
- Clay molding tools or an old teaspoon
- A wooden skewer or toothpick

Directions

1. Roll a small piece of clay (about the size of the tip of your pinkie finger) into a little ball. Flatten the ball slightly so that one side is flat but keep the convex angle of one side. Flatten the top of the resultant shape and scoop it out a little so that you create the rim of the pot.

2. Pinch the other end of the ball slightly so that your pot tapers. Flatten the bottom edge so that your pot's bottom is straight. Make adjustments as necessary so that the shape is right, and then use the skewer/toothpick to make indentations for the rim of the pot. If you like, draw a design on it. Leave overnight to dry. Your embellishments are ready to use.

7. Trendy Key Holder

Materials

- A wooden off cut (ask at your local hardware store, you may not even have to pay for it)
- Pegs or hooks of your choice
- A power drill
- Wooden sealant or paint

Directions

1. Sand the edges of the board so that they are smooth, and then varnish or paint it as you like. Set aside to dry.

2. Drill small holes into the wood at equidistant spaces so that you can easily put the hooks in place. Attach the hooks and then hang on the wall. You are done.

8. Photo Blocks

Materials

- Bits of wood off cuts (big enough to fit your photos onto them)
- Copies of your favorite photos on normal typing paper (the image will be reversed)
- Gel medium
- A suitably sized paintbrush
- Duct tape

Directions

1. You can easily flip your photos on your home computer using image-editing software. Print out your photos onto standard typing paper. Lay your picture, face down, onto the top of the board. Tape into place using the duct tape – this is important because if the paper shifts, your image will be ruined.

2. Check what the instructions are for your gel medium. Generally speaking, you will need to apply the medium to the back of the print so that it becomes saturated. You will then normally need to gently rub the back of the print to allow the image transfer to take place. The next part is tricky. You need to peel off the back paper without disturbing the design. Leave to dry properly and finish with a coat of Modge Podge if you want to.

9. Fun Pillowcases

Materials

- A plain or patterned pillowcase that needs sprucing up
- A length of pompom trim (enough to fit all the way around the outside of the pillowcase)
- A sewing machine
- Coordinating sewing thread

Directions

1. Removing the seams of the pillowcase is tedious but it is worthwhile in the end. The trim will be better secured. The only seams that you do not need to remove are those on the side where the pillowcase opening is.

2. Take the top layer of the pillowcase and lay it down, right side facing up. Lay the pompom trim along the seam line so that it is evenly spaced. It should be laid facing into the center of the pillowcase so that when the pillowcase is turned the right-side out, it will be on the right side.

3. Lay the bottom of the pillowcase on top of this, right side facing down, and line it up with the other seam. Pin it in place, remembering to leave the side with the pillowcase opening as it is. Sew all three layers together on the three "closed" sides of the pillowcase. On the fourth side, sew the pom-pom trim into place on only the top layer of the pillowcase.

10. Hot Pad with A Difference

Materials

- Flat and smooth river pebbles of an even size
- Felt (a heavy weave one)
- A piece of strong cardstock
- Craft knife/ scissors
- A hot glue gun

Directions

1. Cut the felt and cardstock to the size that you want the hot pad to be. You will need two pieces of felt and one of cardstock. Sandwich the card between the two pieces of felt and glue together.

2. Take the pebbles and lay them all over the felt. Try to cover as many of the gaps as possible. You want to cover the felt completely. Glue them in place and you are done.

11. Coasters with A More Rustic Feel

Materials

- A pencil
- Stiff cardstock
- A ruler
- Yarn in the colors of your choice
- A craft knife or scissors
- A tapestry needle

Directions

1. Measure out spaces along the long sides of the cardstock. You want them about 1/8 inch apart. Notch the cardstock according to these marks. Lay your yarn, using the notches as a guide. You now have your warp threads and can start weaving.

2. These threads will be the vertical threads in the finished piece. Weave the yarn horizontally along these threads – start by going up over the first thread and going under the second one, etc. Carry on until there is no longer any space left and the cardboard is completely covered. Your coaster is ready.

12. Make Plain Glassware Special

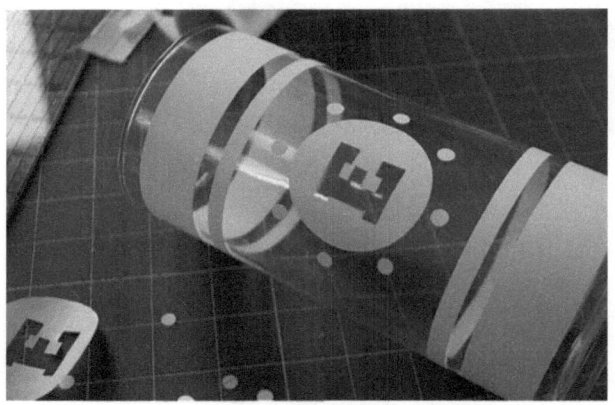

Materials

- Glasses or any other type of glassware
- Etching paste
- Clear contact paper
- A design

Directions

1. Trace a design onto the contact paper and cut out the spaces that you want to appear etched. Any piece of glass exposed to the etching paste will become frosted, so cover area that you do not want etched with contact paper.

2. Adhere the contact paper to the glassware as you like, and apply the etching paste. Set aside to dry. Once dry, rinse off using running water, and remove the contact paper. Clean off any sticky residue and you are done.

13. Make Your Own Joy

Materials

- Wooden letter cutouts that spell out "joy," or whatever word or name that you want
- Modge Podge
- Pretty paper
- A craft knife or scissors
- Embellishments of your choice

Directions

1. Lay each of the letters flat and trace them onto the front of your pretty paper.

2. Cut out the designs and then stick them to your letters with the pattern facing up. Apply a layer of Modge Podge and set aside to dry. Apply a second layer of Modge Podge at a 90-degree angle to the first and set aside to dry. Decorate with embellishments if you want to. Your letters are ready for use.

14. Pompom Mania

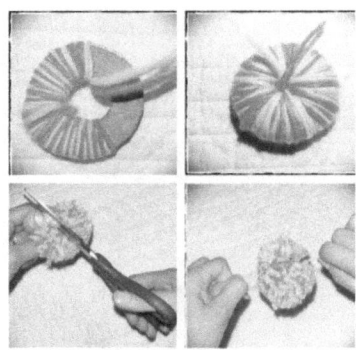

Materials

- A piece of stiff cardstock
- A pair of scissors or a craft knife
- Yarn in the color of your choice

Directions

1. Cut two equal-sized circles from the cardstock and cut out the center of each piece as well. The bigger the pompom you need, the bigger your rings should be. It is important to get the middle hole exactly in the center or your pompom will come out lopsided.

2. Hold the rings together and tie a piece of yarn around them. Wrap the yarn around the rings, making sure to cover them well. The more layers of yarn you use, the fuller your pompom will be.

3. Cut the wool around the outer edge of the ring and hold firmly in place. Discard the cardstock. Take a second piece of yarn and wrap this midway around your yarn. Wrap a few times for good measure so that it is secure. Fluff out the pompom.

15. Decorative Appliqué

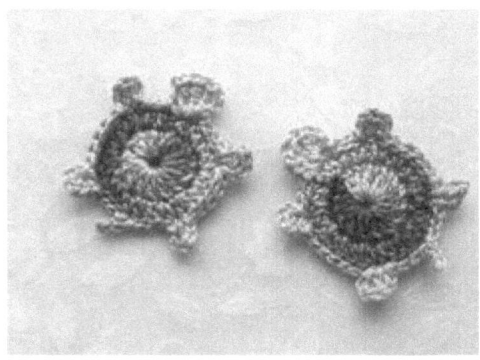

Materials

- Knitted shapes to use as decoration
- A needle with a fairly large eye and sharp point
- Sewing thread for tacking
- Yarn in coordinating colors
- The item of clothing that you are decorating

Directions

1. Make sure to iron your shapes so that they are not wrinkled. Put in place on your item of clothing, and tack into place.

2. Sew around the edges of the shapes using a coordinating yarn and a decorative stitch such as blanket stitch.

16. Stencil Crazy

Materials

- A piece of acetate to make the stencil
- Your chosen design
- Duct tape
- Acrylic paint in the colors of your choice
- A craft knife
- A self-healing mat
- A stencil brush
- Water-soluble pen

Directions

1. Place your design under the acetate sheet and tape in place so that the design doesn't move. Trace onto the stencil using a water-soluble pen. Cut out the shape using your craft knife, taking care to follow the design. Set the design where you want it and tape in place again – this time using cello-tape.

2. Load the brush with a little of the paint. If you use too much, the paint will smudge.) Apply by either using a stippling motion or a circular motion until the area is covered to your satisfaction. Leave to dry. Apply a second coat of paint if necessary.

17. Coiled Bowls with A Difference

Materials

- Rope–cotton or sisal or make your own from scraps of fabric
- A sewing machine
- Coordinating thread

Directions

1. Set your sewing machine to a long zigzag stitch, and coil your rope as you sew it to form the base of the bowl.

2. Do the same with the sides of the bowl, adding more coils until you have the size you want.

18. Scrappy Spice

Materials

- A scrap booking album
- Pretty patterned paper and cardstock
- An acid-free adhesive
- Various embellishments
- Craft punches
- Scissors, a craft knife, or paper trimmer
- An acid-free pen

Directions

1. Settle upon the theme for your album and select the photos accordingly. Choose the very best photos, and cut them to size if necessary.

2. Choose your background color based on your theme or a color that you picked up from the photos. Create a background using cardstock in this color, and adhere your photos in the desired layout. If you like, choose a suitably colored mount for your photos to frame them. Now you have the basic layout. It is now up to you to decorate your pages however you want.

19. Lovely Translucent Kite

Materials

- Construction paper in black (a whole sheet as big as you want your kite to be)
- Construction paper strips in black (about ½ inch wide)
- Tissue paper in various colors
- Clear contact paper
- A length of ribbon, string, or yarn
- Scrap pieces of construction paper in different colors

Directions

1. Cut the whole sheet of construction paper into the shape of a kite. Draw a 1" border on the outside of the paper, and cut out the center. Snip the tissue paper into small pieces. Make different shapes for variety. Unroll a piece of contact paper big enough to fit your kite frame on and take off the backing. The adhesive side should be facing up.

2. Start by placing your frame so that it is stuck down securely. Take the black strips of paper and create a design using these. This will be like the lead that you see in stained glass windows.

3. Set out the pieces of tissue paper so that you get the design that you like. Place another piece of contact paper over the first, sticky side down, so that all the paper is enclosed. Cut out the outside of the kite. Make a string for the kite with the yarn, and decorate with the construction paper scraps.

20. Pretty Easy Bracelet

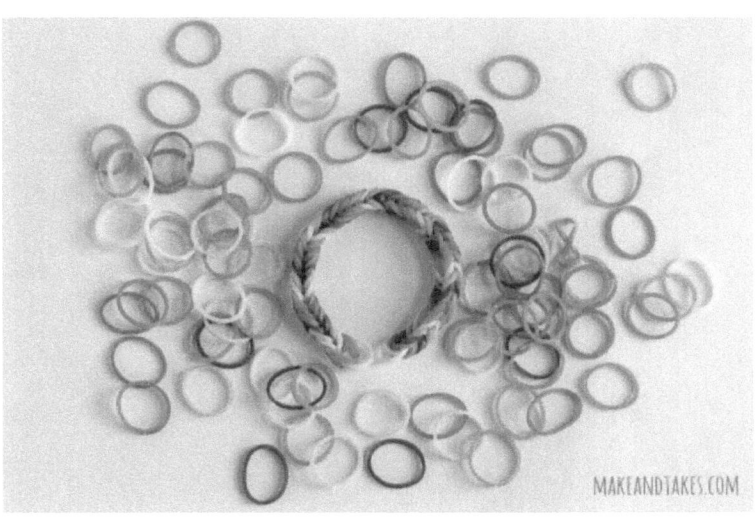

Materials

- Loom bands in the color of your choice
- A loom and hook
- S clips

Directions

1. Follow the instructions that came with your loom to learn how to join the bands together. Carry on in this manner until the band is long enough to fit around your wrist.

2. Add on the S clip to make fastening and unfastening the bracelet easier.

21. Scrubbies For Your Bath

Materials

- Yarn suitable for crocheting
- A small gauge crochet hook
- A pair of scissors

Directions

1. Create a slipknot and chain 4 as your foundation row. Create a slipstitch into the first chain so that it forms a circle. Chain 2. This replaces the initial double crochet stitch for the round. Do 11 double crochets into the circle created. Create a slipstitch into the uppermost point of your first chain.

2. Chain 2 and double crochet into the first gap created in the first round. Chain 1 and then double crochet into the second gap. Repeat into each of the following gaps. Continue in this manner until your circle is big enough and then cast off.

22. Family Memory Box

Materials

- A plain box or square tin
- Acrylic paint
- Modge Podge
- Paint brushes
- Photos that will mean something to you
- Coordinating embellishments
- Mementos that mean something to you

Directions

1. Paint the outside of the box or tin with the paint in order to spruce it up a bit. Apply two coats of paint, leaving it to dry between each coat. Set your image on the lid of the box in the position that you like. When you are satisfied, glue it in place using the Modge Podge. Smooth it out so that there are no bubbles, and brush on another layer of Modge Podge. Set aside to dry.

2. Cover with another layer of Modge Podge and set aside to dry. Embellish as you like. Get creative. Use seashells or sand collected from your latest holiday. Put mementos and photos into the box, and you are done.

23. Dried Flower Cards with A Difference

Materials

- Various dried flowers (dry them with silica so that they keep their shape and color)
- A hot glue gun and a stick adhesive
- Cardstock
- Fine-liners in different colors
- A small circle to use as a template

Directions

1. Fold your cardstock so that it forms a card. You are now going to create a picture of a topiary. Place your circle template about three quarters up from the bottom of the card. Take a card stock paper and draw a topiary head keeping the jar lid as a stencil.

2. Using the hot glue gun, apply a thin layer of glue into the circle. Sprinkle dried flowers over the glue, and press them into place. Do this carefully, since the glue is hot. Leave it to dry and then shake off the excess flowers. Using the fine-liners, draw a stem and pot for the topiary. Add in some grass on the ground as well, and you are done.

24. Made in Minutes Flower Bouquet

Materials

- A few glue dots
- Scraps of ribbon
- Pipe cleaners in different colors – one flower takes 6
- Florist's wire or long green pipe cleaners to use as stems
- A small pot or jar to "plant" your flowers in
- Dried rice, to which you have added green food coloring, to act as the soil in the pot

Directions

1. Decorate the "pot" using some ribbon, and then pour the rice into it. Bundle 6 pipe cleaners of the same color together and tie a green pipe cleaner or piece of florist's wire around the center to secure it. This will form your stem.

2. You will now have 12 separate strands. Curl each one so that they make a flower shape. Tie off at the base and arrange the "petals" as you like them. Arrange your flowers in your pot.

25. Upcycled Bottles

Materials

- A bottle of water, labels removed, with only about a quarter of the water left
- Different color of glitter
- Glitter glue
- Embellishments for the outside of the bottle
- A hot glue gun

Directions

1. Pour the different colors of glitter into the bottle. Fill the remainder of the bottle with the glitter glue.

2. Check the effect to make sure it is what you want. Add more glitter if needed. Embellish the outside of the bottle using the glue gun.

26. Happy Cards

Materials

- Plastic googly eyes
- Crayons in bright red and orange
- A black sharpie
- Hot glue and a glue stick
- Cardstock in a sky-blue color, halved
- A yellow cupcake liner

Directions

1. Place the cupcake liner at the top of the cardstock so that it is half on and half off the page. Trace around the edges. Leaving that section blank, decorate the card with rays of red and orange. These will be the sunrays.

2. When satisfied, glue the wrapper "sun" in place. Put the googly eyes on your sun and draw on a mouth and nose. Add a phrase like, "You are my sunshine," inside the card.

27. A New Way to Decorate Clay Pots

Materials

- Flower pots in various sizes – terracotta or clay are best
- An old crocheted doily, a piece of lace trim, or a pretty ribbon
- An airbrush and paints (alternatively, get a spray applicator and thin your acrylic paints down enough to allow you to spray them on)
- Old newspaper or magazine pages
- Masking tape

Directions

1. Start by working on the rim of the flower pot. Wrap the remainder of the pot with the newspaper, and tape it into place so that no paint gets to it at this stage.

2. Place your trim or lace in place on the rim and attach it using tape. Using your spray applicator or airbrush, apply a thin layer of color and leave it to dry. If needed, apply a second coat.

3. Only remove the lace when the paint is dry and repeat the process to cover as much of the pot with these lacy patterns as you like.

28. Memorable Gift Wrap

Materials

- Gift wrap with a simple, uncomplicated pattern
- A special photograph
- Self-adhesive photo corners or acid-free glue
- A mount (optional)
- Embellishments

Directions

1. Wrap your gift as normal. Finish it off by applying the photo corners and setting the photo on top. Alternatively, glue the photo down. If the person wants to keep it, they can simply cut it out of the paper.

2. If using the mount, frame the photo with it, and glue into place. Apply whatever embellishments you like.

29. Educational Butterfly Craft

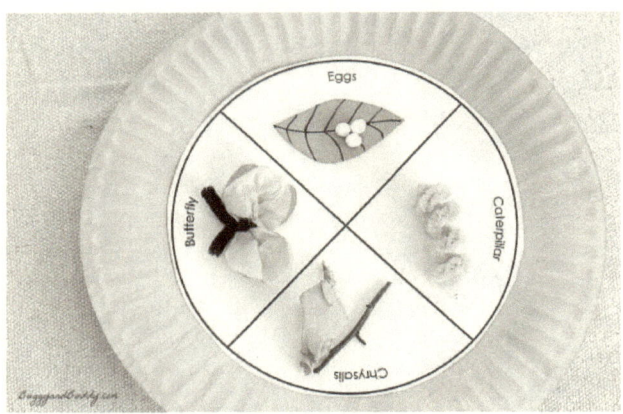

Materials

- A paper plate
- A little bit of green construction paper
- Little white pompoms
- Pretty colored tissue paper
- Different colored pipe cleaners – at least one in black
- Pencil
- Black crayon or permanent marker in black
- Liquid adhesive
- A pair of scissors
- A little twig
- A printed copy of the life cycle of the butterfly that will fit on the paper plate (look online for this)

Directions

1. Cut the printed copy of the life cycle of the butterfly to size so that it fits in the center of your plate. Cut a piece of green construction paper into the shape of a leaf. Glue on two or three of the pompons and glue your leaf and eggs to the front of the plate next to the section on the life cycle dealing with eggs.

2. Take two green pipe cleaners and wrap them tightly around a pencil, while simultaneously twisting them together. This is going to be your caterpillar. Take the small twig and glue it to the rim of the plate next to the section about chrysalises.

3. Cut a rectangular bit of tissue paper measuring 3" x 2". Twist both the top edge and the bottom edge to roughly form the shape of a chrysalis. Glue it in place so that one end looks as though it is hanging onto the twig.

4. Choose colorful tissue paper for the butterfly. Use two contrasting colors. Cut two rectangles that measure 2.5" x 2". Round off the outside edges and stack them together. Using the black pipe cleaner, make the body of the butterfly. Wrap it around the center so that the paper is secure. Glue the butterfly to the plate, and you are all done.

30. DIY Coloring Book

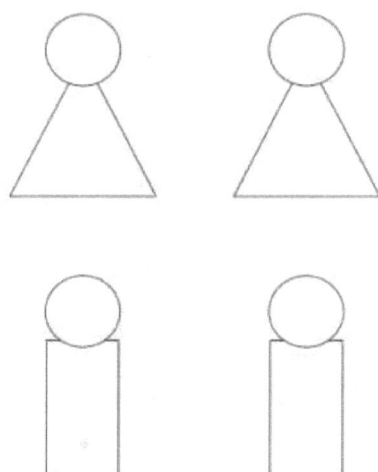

Materials

- Pens, crayons, or colored pencils
- A4 sheets of typing paper
- Staples or a needle and thread
- Internet connection
- A3 sheet of construction paper

Directions

1. Look online for free printable coloring pages. Find a nice selection and print them all out. Fold the construction paper in half. This will be the cover of your book.

2. Stack the pages one on top of the other in between the two layers of construction paper so that they form a book shape. Either secure the book using staples or the needle and thread. Color to your heart's content!

31. Upcycled Egg Boxes

Materials

- Different colors of acrylic paint
- A cardboard egg carton
- A few straws – these will be the stems
- A pair of scissors
- A hot glue gun
- A paintbrush
- Small yellow pompoms

Directions

1. Cut out four of the sections of the carton for each flower. Paint each section in a different color. Using your hot glue gun, attach the straw to the center of the underside of the sections that you cut out.

2. Place a small pompom in the center of each flower that you have just created.

32. Home Grown Crystals

Materials

- Pipe cleaners in colors of your choice
- A jar with a wide mouth (an old jam jar is ideal – it should be a glass container though)
- Water that has been brought to a boil (do not let it cool too much)
- Borax
- A piece of string
- A couple of pencils

Directions

1. Make whatever shape you like from the pipe cleaner and tie a piece of string to it. The other end of the string should be tied to one of the pencils.

2. Place the boiling water into the jar, and mix in 3 tablespoons of Borax. Stir until fully dissolved. Put the pipe cleaner into the jar and suspend the pencil over the mouth of the jar. Set aside at least overnight. The next day you will be able to see crystals on the pipe cleaner.

33. I Love a Ladybug Card

Materials

- A piece of cardstock, folded into the shape of a card (or a blank card)
- A pair of scissors
- Black and red pretty paper
- A black permanent marker
- A glue stick
- A large circle craft punch
- A little heart craft punch

Directions

1. Punch out two circles (one red and the other black). Cut the red circle in half. Punch out six hearts (four in black and two in red).

2. Glue the black circle in the center of the front flap of your card. Glue the red semi-circles over this, at an angle to one another so that it looks like the wings of a ladybug.

3. Use the two red hearts to mark the antenna of the ladybug. Glue two of the black hearts onto each wing of the ladybug. Write in a cute caption, and you are done.

34. Flowers Using Leftover Yarn

Materials

- Green pipe cleaners
- Tacky glue or a hot glue gun
- Cardstock in a coordinating color to the yarn
- A pair of scissors
- Scraps of yarn

Directions

1. Make a yarn pompom, but instead of wrapping the center with yarn, wrap the end of a pipe cleaner around it once and glue it into place.

2. Fluff out the pompom as usual and place it in a vase.

35. Fun Fridge Cups

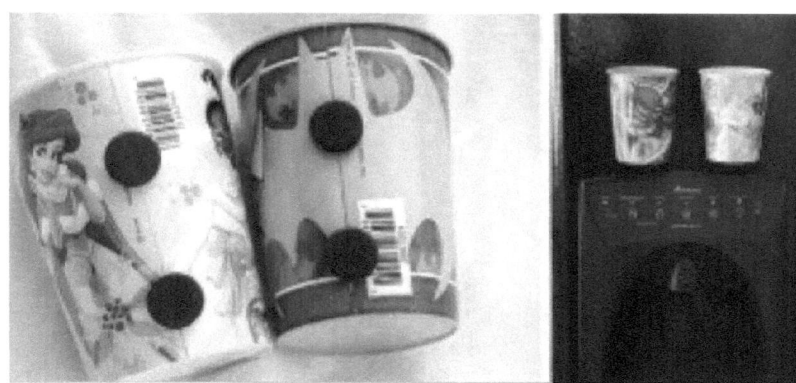

Materials

- A hot glue gun
- 2 lightweight plastic cups
- 2 strips or blocks of magnets

Directions

1. Using your hot glue gun, secure the magnet to the side of the cup well.

2. Set aside to dry. You can use your cups to hold lightweight things.

36. Make Your Own Pump for Water Balloon Fights

Materials

- An empty plastic bottle with a pump handle (a soap dispenser works well)
- Acrylic paints
- Embellishments of your choice
- A hot glue gun or glue stick
- A paintbrush

Directions

1. Paint the bottle with 2 layers of paint, allowing each to dry thoroughly before applying the next layer.

2. Attach whatever embellishments you like (anything that is heavy will need to be applied with the hot glue gun). Add water to the bottle as necessary, and use it to fill your balloons.

37. All Stitched Up

Materials

- An awl
- A daisy flower template
- A cork board or self-healing mat to press on
- Thread that coordinates with your card
- A sewing needle
- A piece of cardstock, folded to make a card
- A suitably-sized envelope

Directions

1. Lay the template down on the front flap of the card, and clip it into place. Open the card and place it on top of the board. Using the needle, punch evenly spaced holes along the outside lines of the daisy template.

2. Knot the thread and sew along the holes that you just punched, joining the holes using the thread. Carry on until you are happy with the pattern. Use different colors with your thread to paint a more realistic picture.

38. Make Your Own Journal

Materials

- A sheet of cardstock–big enough to form the cover of your book
- Enough sheets of paper to make pages for the book – they should be slightly smaller than the cover
- A pair of scissors or a paper trimmer
- A hole punch
- Some string, twine, or yarn

Directions

1. Set the card down on the table, wrong side facing up. Stack the white sheets evenly on the card and center them. Fold the whole thing in half, making sure both halves are even.

2. Along the center crease, punch three holes: one in the center and one at either end. Make sure that the holes go through the covers and all the pages.

3. Thread the yarn, string, or twine through the holes a few times to secure the pages together. Knot them off and cut the yarn. Decorate the cover as you like.

39. DIY Puff Paint

Materials

- Acrylic paint
- Elmer's glue
- Saucer
- A paintbrush
- A permanent marker or sharpie in black
- Shaving foam
- Plain paper

Directions

1. Mix equal quantities of the shaving cream and the Elmer's glue on a saucer, and mix in a bit of paint until you get the color that you are looking for.

2. Using your permanent marker, draw your design on the paper. Paint with your DIY puff paint, being careful not to press too hard or it will lose all its puffiness. Set aside to dry.

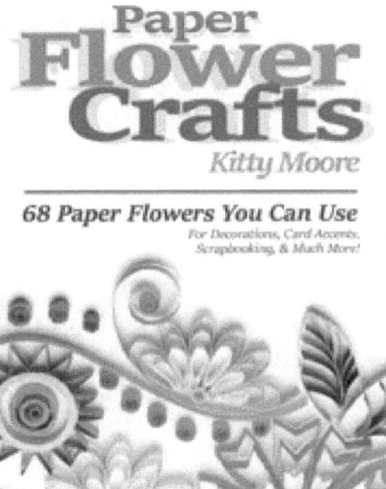

Check out Kitty's books at:

ArtsCraftsAndMore.com/go/books

40. Sunny Sun Macaroni Card

Materials

- Macaroni
- Acrylic paint in sunshine yellow
- Plain white cardstock
- A permanent marker in black
- Elmer's glue or a hot glue gun
- A paintbrush

Directions

1. Decant some of the yellow paint into a saucer, roll the noodles in it, and set it aside to dry.

2. Glue the dried noodles to the paper in a sunbeam pattern. Paint a circle in the center to represent the face of the sun. Draw a face on the sun with the permanent marker.

41. Paper Tissue Flowers

Materials

- Various colors of tissue papers
- A pair of scissors
- A hole punch
- A pretty button
- A pipe cleaner or florist's wires

Directions

1. Cut the paper into circles that are two inches in diameter. You will need 6 "petals" per flower. Stack the circles and find the exact center of the circles. Punch two little holes on either side of this point and center the button over these holes.

2. Thread the pipe cleaner or florist's wire through the first hole, about an inch and half along, catching the papers and button. Thread through the second hole and twist into place in order to secure the flower. Fluff out the tissue paper to form a pretty flower.

42. 4th of July Craft

Materials

- An egg carton with 18 spaces
- A piece of plain paper
- A pair of scissors
- A paintbrush
- Acrylic paint in blue, red, and white

Directions

1. Paint the bottom of the first four eggcups blue. Apply at least two coats of paint. The rest of the eggcups should be painted red and set aside to dry.

2. Using a strip of cardstock or ruler as a stencil, paint stripes over the red. A few coats might be necessary to cover all the red. Draw a star on each of the blue eggcups and set aside to dry.

43. Make Yarn Fireworks for The 4th of July

Materials

- Various pieces of scrap yarn in the colors of your choice
- Elmer's glue
- A pair of scissors
- Fine glitter in silver or gold
- A scrap piece of black paper

Directions

1. Chop up the yarn into pieces ranging from two to three inches each: some longer and some shorter. Dip the pieces of yarn into the glue so that they are coated, and dip them into the glitter. Set them aside to dry.

2. Using the glue, draw the basic design onto your paper and attach the yarn.

44. Little Family of Chickens

Materials

- A piece of scrap paper
- A permanent marker in orange
- Some yellow pompoms in two different sizes
- Elmer's glue

Directions

1. Set out your paper and paste a large pompom as the body of the chicken and the small pompom as the head of the chicken.

2. Draw on the beak and legs using the orange permanent market. Set aside to dry.

45. Xmas Card Holder

Materials

- Toilet paper tube
- Green ribbon
- A set of googly eyes
- A small stapler
- A red pompom for the nose

Directions

1. Cut the antlers from one side of the toilet tube. Use a piece of the ribbon to create a scarf and wrap it to the opposite end of the tube. Staple it into place.

2. Use the pompom as the nose and glue it on. Glue on the eyes as well. Draw on a mouth, and fold the antlers back so that they stick out.

46. Plastic Fantasy Spoons

Materials

- A styrofoam cup
- Acrylic paint
- Bits of tissue paper
- Some disposable spoons
- Pompons
- Adhesive

Directions

1. Draw petal shapes on the tissue paper and cut them out. Glue onto the inside edge of the spoon so that you get a flower shape. Glue in a pompom to cover the center joint and to act as the flower's center.

2. Paint the handle of the spoon green, and paint the cup in a color of your choice. Set aside to dry. Once both have dried, turn the cup upside down and push through the base of the cup.

47. Customized Cork Trivets

Materials

- Cork trivets
- A stencil of your choice
- A pair of scissors or a craft knife
- Acrylic paint in black, silver, or any color you choose
- A foam or stencil brush

Directions

1. Line up your stencil over the trivet, and tape it in place. Using the brush, dab on the paint in a circular motion for a more opaque look.

2. Set aside to dry before removing the stencil and moving on to the next one.

48. Make Your Own Apple Embellishments

Materials

- Pipe cleaners (one red, one green, and one brown)
- A hot glue gun

Directions

1. Shape the red pipe cleaner into an apple shape and glue the ends together.

2. Create a leaf from the green one and a stem from the brown one. (Cut them smaller if necessary). Glue the leaf and stem in place and set aside to dry.

49. Holiday Gift Toppers

Materials

- A few cinnamon sticks about the same size
- A ribbon or twine
- A rubber band
- A hot glue gun

Directions

1. Stack together the cinnamon sticks like logs. Wrap the rubber band around the sticks so that they won't move.

2. Tie the ribbon or twine around the stack in order to hide the rubber band. Make a pretty bow. Glue in place on your gift.

50. Personalized Wrapping Paper

Materials

- Plain brown paper
- A chalk pen

Directions

1. Wrap your gift as normal. Draw whatever design you like to frame your message using the chalk pen.

2. Write your message in chalk pen as well and embellish with doodles.

51. Make Your Own Dish Cloth

Materials

- 1 skein of cotton yarn in a color of your choice
- Size 6 knitting needles

Directions

1. Cast on a total of 44 stitches.

2. Knit one, pull one across and repeat for 48 rows. Cast off.

52. Easy Firework Craft

Materials

- Acrylic paint
- A piece of plain paper
- Paintbrush
- Glitter (optional)

Directions

1. Decant the paint into a saucer and dip the brush in the paint.

2. Dab the brush onto the paper lightly so that you get a firework effect. If you're using glitter, sprinkle it over the paper while the paint is still wet.

53. Waterfall for Your Pond

Materials

- A plain paint tray
- A water pump and hose
- River pebbles and stones with a good shape

Directions

1. Choose a rock to be the focal point. The paint tray is going to form the base of the waterfall. Make sure that the water can easily flow over the lip of it.

2. Set the tray in place at a slightly higher level than your pond. The higher the tray, the longer the waterfall drop will be.

3. Run a hose from the pump to the top of the waterfall. Hide the tray using the rocks.

54. Sharpie Mug Craft

Materials

- A plain mug
- An oil-based sharpie
- Stickers to use as a stencil
- An oven

Directions

1. Stick the stickers on the mug, and draw on your design with the Sharpies. Set it aside to dry.

2. Peel the sticker off and then preheat the oven to 350 Fahrenheit. Bake for half an hour to set the paint.

55. Upcycled Vases

Materials

- Different glass jars out of the recycling
- Sandpaper–120 grit
- Spackle paste
- A craft knife
- Old magazines or newspaper
- Acrylic paint
- Modge Podge
- A paintbrush

Directions

1. Cover the jar with an even layer of spackle paste and set aside to dry. It should be about ¼ inch thick. Sand down as necessary to smooth the edges. Paint as desired, and set aside to dry.

2. Cover with at least two layers of Modge Podge, allowing each layer to dry before painting on the next layer.

56. A "Breath of Fresh Air" Wreath

Materials

- A pre-made blank wreath
- Duct tape
- Baubles or beads
- Nice thick ribbon
- A hot glue gun

Directions

1. Cover up the wreath with duct tape so that nothing shows through.

2. Attach the beads and baubles using hot glue. Cover all available space so that no duct tape shows. Finish it off with a ribbon bow.

57. Decorated Birdhouse

Materials

- A blank birdhouse
- Pages from an old book
- Modge Podge
- Pretty patterned paper
- A sponge brush

Directions

1. Cut pages to fit the sides of the birdhouse. Paint a layer of Modge Podge onto the birdhouse and stick on the pages of the book. Smooth out any bubbles.

2. Cut out pretty flowers and birds from the paper to decorate the birdhouse. Apply using Modge Podge. End with two layers of Modge Podge to seal everything, and you are done.

58. Gloved Doll

Materials

- A single pair of knitted gloves
- Sewing thread in a coordinating color
- A sewing needle
- Stuffing
- A set of black beads to use as the eyes
- Red thread to use as the mouth
- Yarn for the hair
- Ribbon
- A pair of scissors

Directions

1. Straighten out the glove. The middle fingers of the glove will form the legs of the doll. The finger right next to the thumb is where you will start. Slide this finger into the finger of the glove next to it. Repeat with the pinkie finger. You will be left with two fingers and a thumb.

2. Now you need to make the arm hole so that the thumbs end up acting as the arms. The fingers from the second glove need to be sewn together to form the head. Sew the two gloves together at the wrist, leaving enough space to put the filling in. Sew the thumbs into position as the arms.

3. Stuff the doll so that it is nicely full. Add the beads for the eyes, and sew on a mouth and nose. Sew up the opening, and decorate the doll as you like.

59. Winter Wonderland Bow

Materials

- A plastic snowflake
- A wide wire-edged ribbon
- A coordinating piece of ribbon
- A hot glue gun or tacky glue

Directions

1. Cut the wired ribbon so that it is about 14 inches in length. Halve the ribbon to find the center point and then fold each end to this mid-point with a little overlap on either side.

2. Wind the coordinating ribbon around this central point tightly, and secure it using the hot glue. Glue the snowflake into place using a hot glue gun. Add a thin layer of glue and glitter if you like.

60. Festive Table Runner

Materials

- A length of cloth–18 inches x 80 inches
- Craft paint or fabric paint in gold or silver
- Dressmaking scissors
- An iron
- A paint brush

Directions

1. Iron the cloth if necessary, and lay it on a completely flat surface.

2. Dab on polka dots or paint a pretty pattern onto the cloth and set aside to dry. Iron the cloth on the wrong side again to set the paint.

61. Good Old-Fashioned Rock Candy

Materials

- One cup granulated sugar
- A pinch of salt
- 1/2 cup light corn syrup
- Food coloring if you want
- 1/2 teaspoon of peppermint extract
- Parchment paper

Directions

1. Put the corn syrup, sugar, and salt in a pan with a thick base. Bring the mixture to a boil over low or medium heat, stirring continuously. If you have a candy thermometer, let the temperature get to 300 degrees or the "hard crack" stage.

2. Take it off the heat and mix in the peppermint extract. Stir in the food coloring, if using. Mix in well. Line a pan with parchment paper and pour the mixture in.

3. Set aside to cool. When the mixture is completely cool, break up the candy into bite-sized pieces.

62. Retro Gift Labels

Materials

- Crocheted hearts
- Hang tags
- Stickers to write on
- Twine or ribbon

Directions

1. Check online. There are plenty of patterns to make your own crocheted hearts. They are quick and easy to make.

2. Attach the sticker to the heart using the hang tag. Tie to the gift using the twine or ribbon.

63. Planter Using an Old Tire

Materials

- A tire
- 3 x 12-inch pieces of board, cut at a 15-degree angle at both ends (the wood should measure the same on both sides)
- About 200 yards of sisal
- A weatherproof sealant
- Plywood that is ¾ inch thick and big enough to cover the base of the tire
- 2-inch screws
- 2-inch nuts and bolts
- A power drill

Directions

1. Using a 3/8" drill bit, drill four holes through the plywood and into the sidewall of the tire. Secure using the bolts and flip the tire over. Decorate using the sisal. Attach it with the hot glue gun. Attach the boards to the bottom of the tire using the screws, and you are ready to use your planter.

64. Update an Old Vase or Glass

Materials

- A plain glass or vase
- Masking tape
- Spray paint in the color of your choice

Directions

1. Make patterns on the glass using the tape. Any part of the glass not covered by the tape will be painted.

2. Spray the glass and set aside to dry. Once dry, take off the tape, and discard it.

65. Ombre Vase

Materials

- A plain glass vase
- Masking tape
- Three different colors of spray paint (one a shade darker than the first and one a shade lighter than the rest)

Directions

1. Mask off the top two thirds of the vase. Paint the remaining third the lightest color.

2. Before it dries off altogether, remove half of the tape and paint using the second color. Again, before it dries, remove the last of the masking tape and paint on the third shade. Let it dry completely.

66. Pretty Wooden Spoons

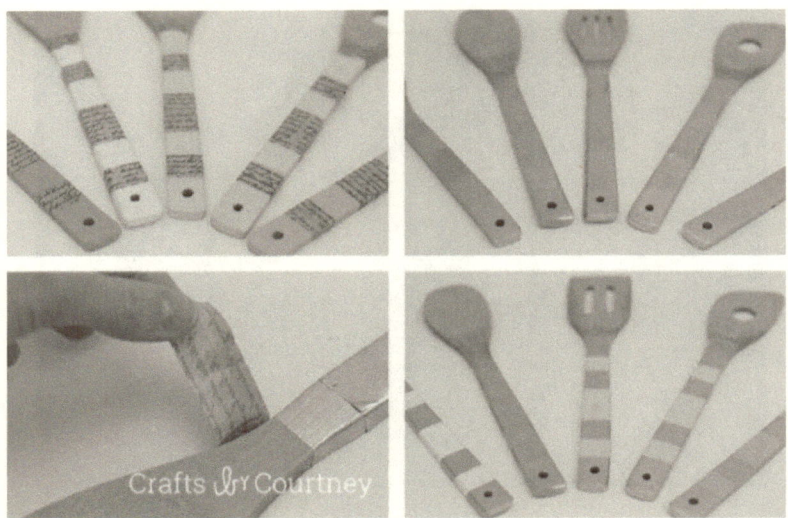

Materials

- A wooden spoon
- Acrylic paint
- Modge Podge that is dishwasher safe
- Masking tape
- Acrylic paint
- A paint brush

Directions

1. Tape up the base of the spoon and tape at intervals along the handle of the spoon. Paint the handle of the spoon. The masking tape will cover the areas not to be painted. Set it aside to dry.

2. Take the tape off and discard. Paint the whole spoon with Modge Podge to seal the paint.

67. Fun Paper Project

Materials

- Watercolor paints
- Plain construction paper
- A pair of scissors
- A paintbrush

Directions

1. Cut the paper into a square about 5 inches x 5 inches. Crumple the paper up so that it is shaped like a ball. Take the first color, paint the whole outer edge of the ball, and allow to dry.

2. Straighten the page out to check the effect. Crumple again and repeat with a second color. Repeat until you get the effect that you want and leave to dry. Iron the page on a low heat in order to smooth out the wrinkles.

68. Paper Bowl with A Difference

Materials

- Strips cut from magazines
- A bone folder or ruler
- A hot glue gun
- Modge Podge
- Paintbrush

Directions

1. Fold each strip using the ruler until they are about 1/4-inch wide. Overlap the ends of the strips and glue into place until you have a good-sized rope. Fold in half again.

2. Coil the "rope" tightly to form the base. The size of the base will determine how big the final bowl will be. Glue each coil into place.

3. Start moving the coil up to form the sides of the bowl and glue as you go along. Continue until the bowl is as big as you want. When complete, seal with a few layers of Modge Podge and set aside to dry.

69. Natural Looking Bottles

Materials

- Thin sisal string or twine
- A plain glass bottle
- A hot glue gun

Directions

1. Starting at the base of the bottle, glue the twine into place and wrap it tightly around the bottle. Make sure there are no gaps.

2. Glue into place and set aside to dry.

70. Cute as A Button Magnets

Materials

- Squares of fabric – 2 inches x 2 inches
- Strong glue
- A button kit
- Small round magnets, a little smaller than the diameter of the button
- A sewing needle and coordinating thread
- Sandpaper

Directions

1. Cover the button as you normally would, but instead of clipping in the back button, sew the fabric down. Alternatively, if you are able to cut the shank of the button off, clip the button into place and cut the shank off.

2. If needed, sand the edges of the shank down. Glue the magnet into place, and set it aside to dry.

71. Custom Paper Bouquet

Materials

- A flower template
- Pretty patterned paper
- Photos that have meaning to you
- Florist's wire or straws

Directions

1. Cut several flowers out of the paper. Cut out the photos so that they cover the center of the flower, and glue them into place.

2. Glue to the florist's wire or straws using a piece of tape to hold them into place.

72. Update Old Sunglasses

Materials

- Clear Modge Podge
- A paintbrush or sponge
- Glitter to match the color of the sunglasses' frames
- Old sunglasses

Directions

1. Cover the temple area of the glasses with a layer of Modge Podge. While it's still damp, sprinkle glitter onto it. Set aside to dry.

2. Finish off with another layer or two of Modge Podge, and allow it to dry thoroughly before use.

73. Easy Canvas Wall Art

Materials

- A block mounted canvas
- A paintbrush
- Different colored and patterned tissue paper
- Modge Podge

Directions

1. Tear the paper roughly into equal sized squares.

2. Arrange the papers on the canvas until you get the desired effect. Glue into place using the Modge Podge. Add embellishments if you like.

74. Crayon Art with a Difference

Materials

- A pack of crayons
- Acrylic paint
- A paintbrush
- A plain glass vase
- A hair dryer or heat gun

Directions

1. Using the acrylic paint, coat the vase completely. Let it dry and, if needed, paint on a second coat.

2. Turn the vase upside down and melt the crayons into place, one at a time. Repeat until you get the desired effect.

75. Fun Noses for Dress Up

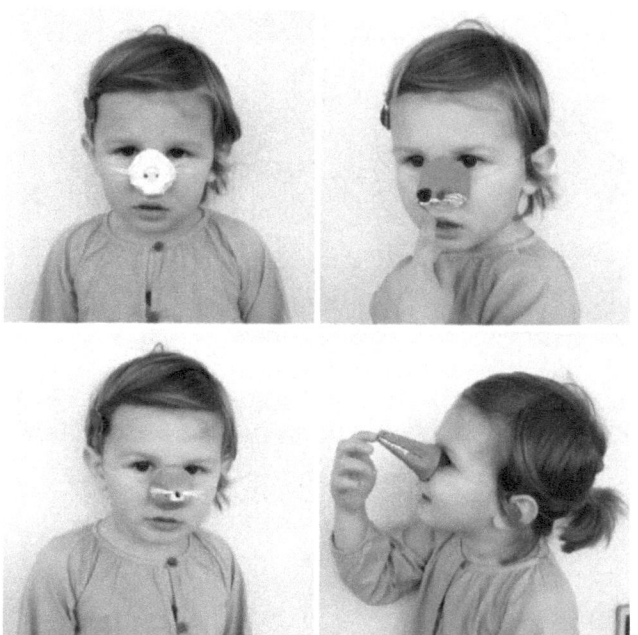

Materials

- An egg carton
- Acrylic paint
- A hole punch
- Elastic string

Directions

1. Cut out each individual eggcup. Using the acrylic paint, cover the entire bottom of the cup. Paint on nose holes. Punch in a small hole on either side of the nose to accommodate the elastic string.

2. Thread the string through one hole, make it big enough to fit around your head, and tie it through the other hole.

76. Retro Pinwheels

Materials

- Pretty patterned paper
- A pair of scissors
- A ruler
- Double-sided adhesive tape
- A hot glue gun
- Scraps of card
- Staples
- A straw (optional)

Directions

1. Cut the paper into strips. The wider they are, the bigger the pinwheels will be. Fold each strip into the center at an angle to get the right shape.

2. Fasten to the center using the double-sided adhesive tape. Staple to the end of the straw. Cover with a circular piece of paper.

77. Keep Your Coffee Warm

Materials

- Bits of leather trim
- A leather punch
- A suede trim
- A coffee cup to use as a template

Directions

1. Cut the trim to fit around the coffee cup with a little gap.

2. Punch the ends of the cuff so that you can thread the suede trim through. You need to be able to lace up the cuff.

78. Easy Origami Craft

Materials

- A square of origami paper
- A ruler
- A pair of scissors

Directions

1. Fold the square in half vertically, then diagonally, and then horizontally to crease and open out again.

2. Fold up the bottom right corner so that it meets the center point. Repeat with the bottom left corner.

3. Fold the bottom up to the center and repeat on the top side. Unfold the top fold and make two equal folds along the diagonal. Flip over and fold the back down again. Repeat on the other side. You now have the base for a boat.

79. Make Your Own Jewelry Bead Cap

Materials

- 2.36-inch soft jewelry wire – 20-gauge is best
- The bead you want to cap
- A bur to smooth the ends of the wire
- Pliers (round nose and flat nose)

Directions

1. Smooth both of the wire ends. Take up one end of the piece of wire with your round nose pliers.

2. Wrap around the tip of the pliers for at least one circle. Continue to wrap it until the wire is completely wound up into a spiral.

3. Push the bead into the center of the spiral to help shape the cap.

80. Rainbow Tissue Flowers

Materials

- Different colors of tissue paper
- A pair of scissors
- A ruler
- A thin wire or ribbon

Directions

1. Fold the sheets of paper in half widthwise, and then again lengthwise, so that there are four layers in a square shape.

2. Cut along the folds to separate out the layers and fold them in half diagonally to make triangles. Fold them in half again. Round off the outer open edges of the flower so that they are curved. You can also use decorative scissors.

3. Repeat with three different sheets of paper, and wrap the bottom edge of the flower so that it is secure. Fluff out the petals.

81. Festive Fall Napkin Ring

Materials

- Decorative paper leaves
- Modge Podge
- Gold or silver glitter
- Scraps of burlap
- A hot glue gun

Directions

1. Apply a thin layer of Modge Podge. While it is still wet, sprinkle glitter over it. Set it aside to dry.

2. Straighten the edges of the burlap so that they are rectangular. Glue the two ends together.

3. Glue a few leaves over the seam of the burlap so it is hidden. Leave it to dry.

82. Decorative Gift Envelope

Materials

- 1 Plain envelope
- Images cut out of old cards
- Brown paper
- Embellishments that you like
- Decorative scissors and plain scissors
- A pencil
- A ruler

Directions

1. Close the envelope and seal it. Take the short edge of the envelope off using the decorative scissors.

2. Decorate the front of the envelope using the brown paper and embellishments.

83. Durable Duct Tape Wallet

Materials

- A role of duct tape
- A ruler
- A pair of scissors

Directions

1. Start with a length of duct tape that is 9 ½ inches long. Lay it on the table with the adhesive side facing up. Cut another piece the same size and lay it on top of the first, sticky side facing down so that it overlaps the first piece about halfway up. Fold the remainder of the strip at the bottom up and over to close off the strip. Make sure there are no bubbles.

2. Flip the strips over and fasten on another strip of duct tape, this time covering the sticky section on the back. Carry on working this way until you have a piece of fabric that is about 7 inches in length.

3. Create pockets in the wallet using the same technique, ensuring that all the adhesive sides are covered. Trim the short sides so that they are completely straight. Cover the edges of the wallet with strips of duct tape and fold the wallet in half.

84. 15-Minute Gift Bag

Materials

- An envelope (however big you want your gift bag to be)
- A paper trimmer or ruler
- A pair of scissors
- A pencil
- Scraps of cardstock
- Embellishments of your choice

Directions

1. Close the envelope and seal it. Cut one of the short sides of the envelope off so that your gift bag has an opening.

2. Cover the back of the envelope with the card scraps so that you cannot see the joins.

3. Add whatever embellishments you wish to add.

85. Ombre Planter

Materials

- Three shades of chalk paint (different tones of the same color)
- An empty tin
- A paintbrush
- Modge Podge

Directions

1. Clean the tin properly and apply a layer of Modge Podge. Leave to dry. Paint the whole tin with the lightest color of chalk paint. Allow it to dry, and paint on a second layer.

2. When the second layer is dry, paint the bottom two thirds of the tin with the second darkest color. Paint a second layer if needed. When that coat is dry, paint the top third of the tin with the darkest color. Repeat if necessary.

86. Easy Easter Floral Bouquet

Materials

- Florist's wire
- Colored eggs that have had the contents blown out
- A hot glue gun
- Flowers or buttons

Directions

1. Make a small hole in the base of the eggshell. Bend the top edge of the wire and push it through the eggshell.

2. Place a dab of hot glue in the base of the eggshell and glue a flower or pretty button onto it.

87. Gift Envelope for Gift Vouchers

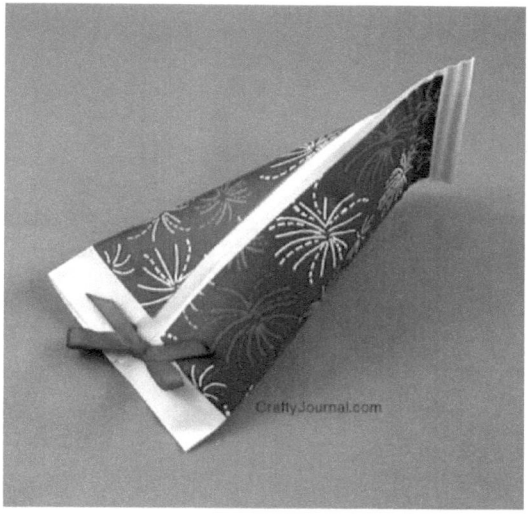

Materials

- An envelope
- Some pretty patterned paper
- A pair of scissors
- A hole punch
- A paper crimper
- Adhesive
- Ribbon or lace to decorate the envelope

Directions

1. Close off the envelope and trim off one of the short ends, about ¼ inch in.

2. Cut a couple of pieces of patterned paper that fit onto the envelope, and glue them into place. Run the bottom inch or so of the envelope through the crimper. Embellish with ribbon or lace.

88. A Pretty Patterned Marquee Sign

Materials

- A marquee love letter kit
- Bits of patterned paper
- A hole punch
- A pair of scissors
- Glue

Directions

1. Lie out the patterned paper along the inside of the marquee, and glue them into place.

2. Make evenly spaced holes with the hole punch. This is where you will insert the lights.

3. Push the lights through. You are done!

89. I Love You Bookmarks

Materials

- Pretty patterned paper
- A bone folder or the back of a spoon to reinforce creases
- A ruler
- A pair of scissors
- A pencil

Directions

1. Cut the paper into pieces that are 5 inches x 2 ½ inches. Fold in half lengthwise. Fold in half widthwise and reinforce the crease. Open them up again.

2. Fold the bottom right edge of the paper up to the center. Do the same on the left. Flip the paper. Fold the top piece down to about 3/8 inches. Crease and repeat the fold on the other side.

3. Fold each of the remaining four corners together so that you end up with a heart shape. Tape the corners down to hold the shape.

90. Quick Striped Canvas

Materials

- A block-mounted canvas
- Acrylic paint in colors of your choice
- Straight edged scraps of paper to use as a template
- Patterned paper
- Adhesive
- A heart template
- White gesso

Directions

1. Using the paper as a template for a straight edge, paint a series of stripes onto the canvas. Leave to dry.

2. Trace around the heart and fill in the heart with gesso. Set aside to dry. Paint the heart in a contrasting color and set aside to dry. Add strips of paper to the canvas as you see fit, and glue them in place.

91. Updated Stone-Finished Pot

Materials

- Stone finish aerosol spray
- A plain terracotta pot

Directions

1. Spray the pot with the stone finish aerosol spray.

2. Set aside to dry.

92. Pretty Fairy Lights

Materials

- Mini plastic disposable cups (enough to cover all the lights)
- Acrylic paint in colors that you choose
- A paintbrush
- Masking tape
- A string of lights

Directions

1. Mask off different strips on each of the cups. Mask off the bottoms of some and the tops of others.

2. Paint a layer of paint on each cup and remove the tape. Make a hole in the base of the cup that the light bulb can fit through. Push the lights through the cups. Hang the string of lights wherever you want.

93. Brighten Your Potted Plants

Materials

- Terracotta pots
- Paintbrushes
- Masking tape
- A selection of neon acrylic paints
- Acrylic craft paint in white

Directions

1. Mask off the bottom half of the pot. Paint the top half of the pots with the neon paints. Choose different colors for each pot. Set them aside to dry. Add another layer if needed. Once they are dry, remove the tape.

2. Paint the rest of the pot with your white paint, again using two coats if needed.

94. Cupcake Liner Flowers

Materials

- Dry black beans
- Cupcake liners in pretty colors
- A hot glue gun
- A skewer
- Green paint

Directions

1. Flatten the cupcake liners, and set them down so that the patterned side is facing up.

2. Glue the beans into the center of the "flower". Paint the skewers green, and set them aside to dry. Put a dollop of glue on the back of your flower and attach to the flat end of the skewer.

95. Beautiful Personalized Tags

Materials

- Pretty patterned paper (plain on the back)
- A tag template
- Tape
- Scissors or a craft knife

Directions

1. Cut the tags from the patterned paper.

2. You can either write a message on the back and attach to a gift or write on the front of the paper in a contrasting color and tape onto containers, etc.

96. Swirl Embellishments

Materials

- Fine Salt
- Food coloring or acrylic paint
- A non-stick silicone mat
- A dropper or straw
- A hot glue gun

Directions

1. Swirl glue onto the silicone mat.

2. While still wet, sprinkle with salt. Drop food color or paint onto the swirls. Set aside to dry.

97. Quick Stamps for Personal Projects

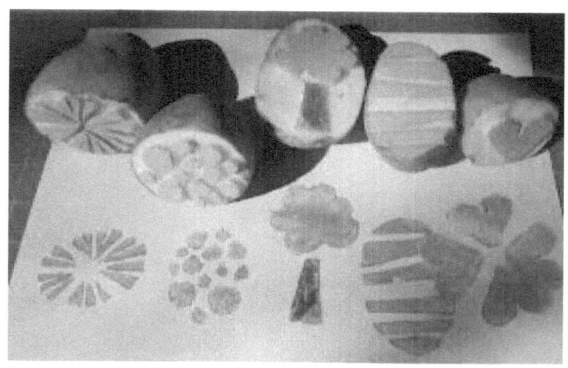

Materials

- A selection of potatoes
- Acrylic paint
- A selection of textured buttons
- Paper
- A paintbrush

Directions

1. Cut the potatoes in half and then carve a basic flower shape out of it. If you don't want flowers, make a different shape.

2. Insert the button into the center of your stamp to create a pretty center.

3. Place the paint in a saucer and dab the potato into it. Spread paint evenly with the paintbrush and then stamp it onto the paper.

98. Oak Tree Crafts

Materials

- Acrylic paints
- Acorns collected from the garden
- A paintbrush
- A pair of scissors
- Green construction paper
- An oak leaf to use as a template
- A hot glue gun

Directions

1. Paint each acorn, and set them aside to dry. Trace some leaves onto the paper, and cut them out.

2. Group the leaves in threes and glue together. Glue a cluster of acorns onto the base. Your decorations are done.

99. Chicken Pix for Younger Kids

Materials

- Shaving cream
- Elmer's white glue
- Yellow acrylic paint or yellow food coloring
- Coordinating patterned paper to make eggs
- Googly eyes
- A pair of scissors

Directions

1. Mix equal parts of glue and shaving cream and color with the paint or food coloring. Dab onto the paper to make the head of the chick.

2. Cut a rough egg shape out of the paper. Cut across the top using serrated edge scissors or cut the top off in a zigzag shape to simulate a hatched egg.

3. Glue the paper eggs under the chick's heads so that it looks like they are hatching. Glue the tops of the eggs around the base of the picture. Glue on the googly eyes.

100. Ribbon Embellishments

Materials

- Strips of ribbon
- A piece of plain paper in a coordinating color
- A glue stick
- Green acrylic paint
- Adhesive
- Buttons

Directions

1. Cut the paper into five flower shapes. Cut or punch circular centers from the paper for the flower center. Cut 5 x 1-inch strips of ribbon.

2. Glue the first bit of ribbon to the center of the circle. Loop the strip over and glue the other end of the strip next to the first end. Do the same for the other strips. Glue on a button to the center so that you can no longer see the ends of the ribbon.

Final Words

Thank you for downloading this book!

I really hope that you have been inspired to create your own projects and that you will have a lot of fun crafting.

I do hope that you and your family have found lots of ways to fill lazy afternoons or rainy days in a more fun way.

If you have enjoyed this book and would like to share your positive thoughts, could you please take 30 seconds of your time to go back and give me a review on my Amazon book page!

I really appreciate these reviews because I like to know what people have thought about the book.

Again, thank you and have fun crafting!

Disclaimer

No Warranties: The authors and publishers don't guarantee or warrant the quality, accuracy, completeness, timeliness, appropriateness or suitability of the information in this book, or of any product or services referenced by this site.

The information in this site is provided on an "as is" basis and the authors and publishers make no representations or warranties of any kind with respect to this information. This site may contain inaccuracies, typographical errors, or other errors.

Liability Disclaimer: The publishers, authors, and other parties involved in the creation, production, provision of information, or delivery of this site specifically disclaim any responsibility, and shall not be held liable for any damages, claims, injuries, losses, liabilities, costs, or obligations including any direct, indirect, special, incidental, or consequences damages (collectively known as "Damages") whatsoever and howsoever caused, arising out of, or in connection with the use or misuse of the site and the information contained within it, whether such Damages arise in contract, tort, negligence, equity, statute law, or by way of other legal theory.

www.ingramcontent.com/pod-product-compliance
Lightning Source LLC
Chambersburg PA
CBHW031124080526
44587CB00011B/1102